Slope
David Wilson

smith|doorstop

Published 2016 by
smith|doorstop books
The Poetry Business
Bank Street Arts
32-40 Bank Street
Sheffield S1 2DS

Copyright © David Wilson 2016
All Rights Reserved

ISBN 978-1-910367-67-4
Typeset by Utter
Printed by Biddles
Climbers on the Kuffner Ridge, Mont Maudit
copyright, Pierre Abramowski www.switzerland-photos.com

Acknowledgements
A few of these poems have appeared before, in *The North*, *Poetry News*, *Rialto*, *Scottish Mountaineer* and the Cinnamon anthology *Journey Planner*. A few others were prize-winners in competitions and first appeared on their web-sites: Poets and Players (twice), Buxton International Festival and the Mountaineering Council of Scotland.

Thanks go, firstly, to Ann and Peter Sansom, their team at the Poetry Business and everyone in the classes of '12 and '14; to Jim Caruth, Jane McKie, Helen Mort, Stuart Pickford and Rosalind Wilson for their generous help; to Pierre Abramowski for permission to use his photo; and, last but not least, to Ian Duhig.

Notes at the back of the pamphlet explain a few climbing terms and other references.

All author income from this pamphlet will be donated to Community Action Nepal, set up by Doug Scott to support the mountain people of Nepal.

smith|doorstop books are a member of Inpress:
www.inpressbooks.co.uk. Distributed by Central Books Ltd.,
99 Wallis Road, London E9 5LN

The Poetry Business gratefully acknowledges the support of Arts Council England.

Contents

5	After Work, Almscliff Crag
6	Feeding the Crow
7	Indoor Weather
8	Crampons
9	In the Balance
10	The Day
11	Falling
12	The Slab
14	Bivouac at Harrisons' Rocks
15	"I love you"
16	Don't Hold Your Breath
17	Summer with Yeats
18	Mallory
19	Expedition, 1972
20	Stob Coire nan Lochan, Winter
21	The Climber
23	In Praise of Sleet
24	Everest
25	A Chinese Student's Journey
26	Sunrise from the Summit of Poon Hill, Nepal
27	Stanage Edge
28	Down
29	Alpine Partner
30	Notes

After Work, Almscliff Crag

Held in place
by drystone walls
green fields bring
my mind to order.

Among scattered boulders
my favourite slab,
mirror-smooth,
a balance problem.

The first move up
gathers me in,
the next becomes
my only fact.

Feeding the Crow
im Dave Knowles

Hughes' Crow explained the world,
your father's early stroke,
America in Iraq.

You translated words into rock,
gritstone cracks which hung in space,
hand-jams that bit our flesh.

You wanted steep, hard, cold,
a printer's landscape of black and white,
and so to Nevis in February,

an unclimbed buttress in a storm.
Crow is loving this, you said.
Your dark eyes shone.

High in a vertical ice-choked groove
your crampons slipped and scraped.
I had no belay worth the name,

prayed to a kinder, weaker god
that we might get out of this alive.
Crow grinned and flew his black flag.

Indoor Weather

Remember the dark moor,
dawn slogs to high crags,
the disappointment of rain.

Remember those times you were gripped,
the fall when half your hexes ripped out,
bruises appearing like storm clouds.

Come in from your grit and granite
to this hall of coloured holds
with calm, conditioned air.

The problems here are well-designed:
blue, black, white, red – various
selves, most of them satisfied.

While cold rain steams the windows
let music play within the walls,
let mats cushion every fall.

Crampons

I thought I'd given you away.
But opening a jiffy bag in the attic,
there you are: same black spikes
and anti-ball plates, same bindings,
not a fumble with straps, rings, buckles,
but the slip of a boot into a bail,
the pull and snap of a clip.

Tell me again about being single-minded,
about couloirs bulging with fat blue ice
and dawn arriving high in the Alps;
how a slope exists at a perfect angle
where it all might kick in again,
on névé so pure your front-points hold
with just the lightest tap of my toes.

In the Balance

You pause beneath a boss of ice
above a thousand feet of space.
The picks of your axes barely bite:
it's bullet hard, black with rock dust.
You've run out forty feet of rope,
placed only an ice-screw and screamer.
You've dreamed of this route for half your life.
Your calves ache. You can't wait long.

Decision time. Weigh the following:-
an abseil retreat to blankets, pasta, beer;
the taste in your mouth if you bottle out;
November at work without a fix;
glimpses of where the pitch might ease;
a face at a window, *Dad come home*,
and you not knowing where you've been
or how to get back from it.

The Day

You reminded me, how years ago on the school run
I said one day we'll just keep driving,
past the railings and bells and latecomers

to see where the day takes us,
perhaps the beach, perhaps back home,
and I'd let you decide when it should be.

It didn't happen but knowing it was enough
you said, the best thing I ever did.
And I wonder if the same is true for me;

perhaps, when nestled among flowers
with the rear door of my limousine shut,
you might ask the man in black

to keep driving, see where the day takes us,
to hills, the sea, or just around the block
like an uncertain bride taking her time.

Falling

So this is you, your matter,
an oyster shell shucked wide.
The doctor points to the screen:
these white spots are the damage.

Now she passes you different names:
currently asymptomatic, no sensory
hallucinations or episodes of déjà vu
yet. Balance likely to go first.

Ten storeys up, a long way in,
you'll leave her office on a tightrope,
a thought you'd carried all your life
vanishing into thin air.

The Slab

This is for Spring ... that you may remember.
– Les Murray

The slab tilted up for five hundred feet or more.
Slate-grey, with veins of white quartz,
it lay in an amphitheatre of rock, split by gullies
that oozed and dripped. All afternoon I'd sat
waiting by a green lake at the slab's foot
for the last climbers to coil their ropes and leave
so I might take it on unseen,
protagonist in my own drama
or making a fool of myself alone.

I tightened my second-hand kletterschue,
slung borrowed rope around my neck,
lifted my arms and touched the rock,
still warm from late sun but now in shadow.
The mountains held their breath.
It was time, time to make my move
and be gone, time to reach for the small flake
I'd studied for hours, to curl fingers round it,
place my boot on the quartz edge and climb,
the slab flowing beneath me, offering its holds,
unrolling in an almost-blur of moving up till
I was higher than the roof of our house,
the science block at school, the church spire,
moving up and up, the lake below shrinking
to a single calm eye. It was time

as it would be time that night to walk
to the edge of heavy-scented pines
beyond all artificial light,
and give thanks to mountains
who'd been generous that day,
and look up at stars fiercer and brighter
than I'd known, pressing down, breathing in,
breathing out, daring me to believe.

Bivouac at Harrisons' Rocks

Leaves turn from green to grey.
On the breeze, a scent of hops.
A star appears. A bat.

Beyond silver birch trees
a train sounds its two-tone horn,
slows for a bend, disappears.

We're fifteen years old
with apple pies, cans of Sprite,
and dreams of the Eigerwand.

Above our ledge a sandstone roof,
below us the drop. Not far
but far enough.

"I love you"

My parents didn't use this phrase,
talked in terms of work to do, and weather
and how they were bringing us up;
despite whispered rows at night
stayed together, held in place by good form.
They were not much given to using 'I'.

Near the end, my father asked a nurse
to bring my waiting mother
to the side-room of his suffering,
having taken ten minutes to stand up
straight, always the military man,
nearly losing his footing.

One has to be brave at a time like this,
he said, taking her hand,
Some journeys must be made alone.
And then, *Thank you for loving me.*
A slight bow and turn, while she cried
in the voice of a young girl,
'Oh my darling'.

Don't Hold Your Breath

I for one didn't mind the delay,
the three hour wait in Costa Coffee
unable to go forwards or back,
watching the departures board
with its silent electronic shiver,
Dublin, Dubrovnik, Kathmandu,
gates closing, gates open,
cancelled flights, final calls,
nothing to do, nowhere to go,
between the in-breath and the out
Split, Rome, Calgary, Seoul,
Carthage, Tyre, Nineveh, Antioch.

Summer with Yeats

Our climb's in a zawn
of Bosigran granite
above turquoise sea;

we're one from the top
of the graded list,
scene of many falls, but

I know the sequence
do not stop to
think this time

each hold finds
me, shapes my
moves. Now. And

now. And now, as
through cold fingers
glittering summer runs.

Mallory

Preserved by cryogenic cold
he's made a statue of himself.
I shouldn't rubberneck but do.

His arms wide and half-raised as if
for victory, or to break his fall;
his back bare, slabbed with muscle,

the skin alabaster-white; right leg
corkscrewed, but otherwise he's perfect,
as if Death had been re-enchanted

after Flanders. He's still attached
to the rope as we are to him:
old hero with your *manly daring*

I do not want to see you explained
but leave you high on the North East Ridge.
How could they bear to turn you over?

Expedition, 1972

After days spent high on the climb
she carries down sanitary pads
to burn on a base camp fire.
The circle of men falls silent.

Here in the Karakoram –
Black Gravel in Turkic –
she walks off their maps
into whiteness

Stob Coire nan Lochan, Winter

Climbing dissolves me in colour,
orange-red blur of heart effort,
blue precision of balancing up.
Ice becomes my picture plane,

the white surface I pattern with marks.
Our line curves up from the drop below
through to the top of our frozen world.
At every point my placements hold.

We rest at the summit. Landscape stills.
Beyond white hills the sun sets
where islands, sky and sea-lochs merge:
I am here again, I am here after all.

We go back the way we came,
share stories in the listening dusk.
Above Stob Coire's silhouette
two stars balance a crescent moon.

The Climber
In Memoriam Wanda Rutkiewicz 1943 – 1992

1961

Wanda tip-toes up a sunlit slab,
curls her fingers round a spike; hesitates,
then reaches for the heart of a chimney-crack,
back-and-foots and jams against its sides.

She's climbing solo. Friends are shocked.
But she's finding all the holds she needs.
Tonight there will be vodka and songs,
Stalin jokes, a dry cave for sleep.

Churches, smokestacks, lamentations
fall away below her into white mist,
Five Year Plans, queues for food, the broken
walls and people in her twice-betrayed house.

She finds a pebble at the top, smooth,
round, containing nothing but itself.
From today she'll build from summits,
snow, ice, a hundred floors of air.

1992

Crouched in a niche carved from snow,
Wanda faces down the Kanchenjunga night,
alone, at twenty-seven thousand feet,
no water, sleeping-bag or stove.

She should have followed her torch-beam
down the breadcrumb trail of ice-axe marks
to fixed ropes, food, warmth. But then
to where? And what end? With who?

Instead, the long Polish night continues.
The blood-red, ash-grey courage
of Winged Hussars, W-hour, Gdansk
keeps alive her eight thousand metres plan.

※

Dawn breaks at minus twenty, silhouettes
Everest, white against grey-blue.
Frost-nipped fingers paw at frozen boots.
Breath comes hard, air burns her throat.

But still she climbs, her steps inches now.
And should we imagine her happy?
The girl who ran a ruined home at five,
the woman who spurned the token slots

on men's expeditions, early Solidarność.
Sheltered by seracs, embalmed in ice,
Wanda will never be found.
The summit wind howls her eulogy.

In Praise of Sleet

Artist of the passing moment,
it floats, falls, dissolves;
isn't deep; doesn't accumulate,
impose a blank year-zero page.
Wouldn't dream of making a scene.

It has no grand plan for transfiguration,
won't stop retreats from Moscow
or you reaching Tesco.
Doesn't want you to lie down and be an angel;
leaves Michael Furey's grave untouched.

Doesn't have fifty names for itself;
no need to fret if it fails to arrive,
to think of fractured Arctic shelves
and polar bears trapped on floes
like double mattresses cast adrift.

It won't haunt you with a melting story
about how you should have left more tracks
in December in Minnesota, or called across
a glistening slope to Marie, 'hold on tight'.
It slips away while Brueghel mixes paint.

Everest

Once it was Chomolungma,
Mother Goddess of the Earth,
a face whose veil rarely lifted,
its whiteness the White Whale's.

Now it's like Elvis near the end,
a giant in a soiled jumpsuit,
blank, useful for percentages,
a sheet from which the music's fled.

A Chinese Student's Journey

My parents told me in my ancestors' time
state examination candidates got papers,
a day to write down everything they knew,
bowls of rice, and, for those doing badly,
silk rope for their more honourable course.

Reading all hours, I thought of a poor boy,
his ticking rope, his parents' broken hearts.
I studied engineering, but still we learned
Xu Zhimo's 'Leaving Cambridge Again'.
I dreamed of its river shaded by willows.

Sometimes when I study through the night
I think of Newton doing the same nearby;
and of my mother, unable to write her name.
Did I tell you when developers stole our land
she sold her hair to buy my school books?

Sunrise from the Summit of Poon Hill, Nepal

One of the finest anywhere, I'd read,
an experience of the sublime,
and listed in the top hundred
of *A Thousand Things to Do Before You Die*.

We met Mary-Ann in the mountain hut,
from Massachusetts via Madrid.
She worried that the West was stuffed.
We moved on to Buddha and cures for the shits.

Crowds climbed up in darkness and cold.
A line came back from Coleridge,
I will clamber through clouds and exist.
'Dawn will be useless', a Swiss guy moaned,

'I forgot my polarising filter'.
The sun rose; turned hill-tops gold.
Mary-Ann lit a cigarette and frowned,
'What the fuck is meant to happen now?'

.

Stanage Edge

Summer's returned for one day only,
blue sky, no wind, mist in the valleys,
bracken bronzing every hill,
the Edge's gritstone silver in the sun.
Rock warm to touch. But holds won't sweat.

I check my harness, knots and rack,
lay away, step high and up again to poise
off-balance, wriggle a cam into place,
then smear a slab, heels low, until
a crack grips my outstretched hand.

We linger on the edge. Smoke rises
straight up from the chimney at Hope.
It's not a day to hurl ourselves against
but for dancing with, to feel alive
on *Black Slab, Inverted V, Goliath's Groove.*

And it will light the long edge in our minds,
where name after name spells a life,
Flying Buttress and *Left Unconquerable,*
holds we could trust to always be there,
winds which threw every word away.

Down

We've had our fill of *edge* and *jagged* and carrying
weight. How good to be back on flat ground,
an Alpine village, tables under the stars,
pizza stringing up to our mouths,
glasses of red leading us south.

Who knows what starts us laughing, perhaps
Paddy's joke about three dogs at the vet's
or Hilary quoting her dad's secret diary
but it all follows in one mass,
our lives, whatever possessed us.

Eyes stream, we gulp for air,
our laughter tonight a funnel
through which everything passes,
everything that's happened,
everything that will.

Alpine Partner

I was thinking of glaciers as metaphors,
you knew the car park's exit code.
And you'd practised techniques
for rescue from a crevasse,

to dig a T slot, bury your ice-axe,
attach our *micro-traxion* gadget,
then fix the rope as a Z-haul
across the sweating surface, so that inch

by inch you heaved me up when I fell,
up from that cold place – its white walls
and longing, fins of green ice, pale blue caves,
darker blue depths beyond saying.

Notes

Climbing terms

Anti-ball plates: sheets of plastic fitted to crampons to stop snow building up, which can turn crampons into clogs!
Cam: a device fitted into cracks to protect a lead climber. It has spring-loaded metal cams which grip the rock
Hex: hexagonal metal wedges of various sizes, fitted into cracks to protect a lead climber
Névé: snow which has been through freeze-thaw cycles resulting in a firm surface that's good for ice-axe and crampons
Micro-traxion gadget: a pulley that locks the rope, capturing what's gained as a climber is hauled from a crevasse.
Rack: the collection of climbing equipment used to protect a climb.
Screamer: a sling which has stitches designed to rip and thereby absorb the energy of a fall. Typically used with doubtful ice-screws.

Notes on individual poems

'Feeding the Crow'
The title nods to Al Alvarez's book *Feeding the Rat*, and the last line echoes Ted Hughes' poem 'Crow Blacker Than Ever'.

'Mallory'
In 1999, an expedition searched for, and found, Mallory's body. To many in the climbing community, his body was treated with disrespect as it was turned over and searched for clues about whether he and Irvine reached the summit on their 1924 Everest expedition.

'A Chinese Student's Journey'
Many pupils in Chinese schools learn Xu Zhimo's poem 'Leaving Cambridge Again'.

'The Climber'
Wanda Rutkiewicz had a deeply difficult childhood, her family torn apart by the Nazi occupation of Poland and then tragedies during the Soviet era. She took on responsibility for the household budget at five years old. A great mountaineer, her ambition was to climb all fourteen eight thousand metre peaks. See, for example, *Caravan of Dreams* by Gertrude Reinisch and *Freedom Climbers* by Bernadette McDonald.

'In Praise of Sleet'
Michael Furey is a character in *The Dead* by James Joyce.